# W▓▓▓▓e
## and the
# Dog Show

## By
# Roger Priddy

# Gabe, Teddy and Wallace are best friends.

**Wallace is a friendly dog.**

# Gabe, Teddy and Wallace go everywhere together.

**Wallace hates
being left alone.**

# He howls and howls.
# It is very embarrassing.

# When Gabe throws sticks in the park,

# Wallace runs away with the stick.

And doesn't come back
when you call him!

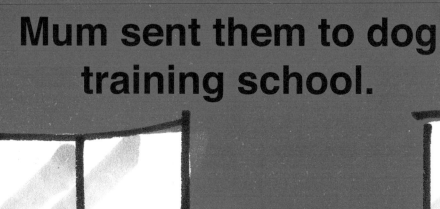

# Mum sent them to dog training school.

But Wallace just wanted to play and bark.

# But they kept going.

And Wallace soon got the
idea. The treats helped!

**Then one day, Gabe saw a sign in the park.**

# On the day of the fair he gave Wallace a bath.

**Wallace shook himself dry.
Then Gabe brushed him.**

# Finally it was time for the show.

Gabe was excited.
Wallace was a bit nervous.

# Gabe and Wallace lined up for the judge.

# Wallace was being very well behaved.

# But then Wallace started to howl!

# He jumped up and licked the judge.

# He crashed into a table.

# And knocked over a vase of flowers and the cup.

# Then he chewed one of the flowers.

# And finally did something bad in the cup!

**Everybody laughed.**

# The judge picked the three best dogs.

# Sadly, Wallace was not one of them.

# But he did make lots of friends.

# And Dad said that was better than winning.